A BRIEF HISTORY OF
NAPOLEON BONAPARTE

Emperor, Exile, Eternity

SCOTT MATTHEWS

Victory belongs to the most persevering.

- Napoleon Bonaparte

Contents

Introduction   ix

1. Corsican Roots: The Making of a
   Revolutionary (1769-1785)   1
2. The Path to Power: Ambition and
   Revolution (1785-1799)   7
3. Ascension of an Emperor: From
   Coup to Coronation (1799-1804)   21
4. The New Empire: Battles and
   Rule (1804/1805-1807)   31
5. Personal and Professional Life:
   Turmoils and Transition (1808-
   1810)   39
6. The Russian Campaigns: The
   Begin of the Fall (1810-1813)   45
7. The Turning Tide: From Moscow
   to Elba (1813-1815)   53
8. Hundred Days and Waterloo: The
   Last Stand (1815-1840)   59
9. Veiled in Mystery: the Enigma of
   Napoleon's Demise   65
10. The Lasting Legacy: Continued
    Influence after Death   69

Conclusion   79
Bonus   83
References   93

Introduction

Embark on an extraordinary journey through the annals of history with *A Brief History of Napoleon Bonaparte: Emperor, Exile, Eternity* by Scott Matthews. This compelling narrative unravels the captivating saga of Napoleon Bonaparte, a man whose life echoed across the ages.

From the rugged landscapes of Corsica to the pinnacle of power as the Emperor of the French, Napoleon's life unfolds in these pages with a blend of meticulous research and storytelling prowess. Beyond the battlefield, this book delves into the intricacies of his character —his ambitions, passions, and moments of vulnerability—painting a nuanced portrait of one of history's most complex figures.

Set against the backdrop of the 19th century, a time of revolutionary fervor and profound change, Napoleon's story transcends the boundaries of a conventional biography. This isn't merely a recounting of events but a vivid exploration of the societal, political, and personal forces that molded his destiny.

As you traverse the chapters, witness the strategic brilliance behind his military conquests, feel the pulse of revolutionary reforms in France, and discover the man behind the legend. *A Brief History of Napoleon Bonaparte* weaves historical accuracy seamlessly with engaging storytelling, ensuring an immersive experience for readers of all backgrounds.

The narrative unfolds like a captivating tapestry, revealing the layers of Napoleon's legacy and the indelible marks he left on the world stage. Whether you're a history enthusiast, a biography connoisseur, or simply curious about the echoes of a bygone era, this book promises a unique and enlightening voyage through the life of Napoleon Bonaparte.

ONE

Corsican Roots: The Making of a Revolutionary (1769-1785)

In the year 1769, amidst the rugged landscape of Corsica, a child was born to the noble families of Buonaparte and Ramolino. He was named Napoleon Bonaparte, a name destined to echo throughout history. The island, freshly claimed by France, instilled in him a unique blend of Italian nobility and Corsican spirit, setting the stage for a life marked by extraordinary duality.

Napoleon's early years were spent in the ancestral Casa Buonaparte, a grand building established by  his great-great-grandfather, Giuseppe, in 1682. This house, later known as Maison Bonaparte, witnessed the shaping of a young Napoleon, under the strong influence of his mother Letizia.

The young Bonaparte's world was one of political upheaval and cultural richness. His parents, Carlo and Maria Letizia, deeply involved in the Corsican struggle for freedom, instilled in him a profound sense of identity. His father, initially a supporter of the Corsican leader Pasquale Paoli, later changed his allegiances, perhaps, instilling in young Napoleon the complex dance of politics and principle.

At the tender age of nine, the call of destiny led Napoleon out from his island home. He was sent to France, to a religious school in Autun, and then to the military academy at Brienne-le-Château. One of the key figures who played a pivotal role in facilitating Napoleon's admission to the military academy, despite his family's lack of financial resources, was the French Governor. He was a friend of Napoleon's mother and significantly contributed to Napoleon's early military education. In Brienne-le-Château, among the sons of the French elite, Napoleon's Corsican roots set him apart. His accent, his modest background, and his pride in his heritage isolated him, yet due to these very trials he turned to his studies with resilience and fervor.

In these formative years, the Age of Enlightenment[1] was at its peak. The age with its emphasis on reason and challenge to the old order, resonated deeply with Napoleon. He absorbed his minds to the lessons of mathematics, history, and geography, each discipline sharpening his innate strategic and analytical powers. Despite initial challenges, he also mastered the French language, adding to the languages of Corsican and Italian. His teachers, with whom he established a great image, recommended him to join artillery, a prestigious branch in the military.

He graduated from the school at the age of fifteen, and went to École Militaire in Paris. At this school, his Corsican heritage once again made him stand out. And he had to face the adversity of his father's death due to cancer, yet despite that he thrived, becoming the academy's first Corsican graduate, with commendations from the esteemed Pierre-Simon Laplace after only one year.

In 1785, after graduating, in an environment rife with political and social shifts in Europe, Napoleon became a lieutenant in the La Fère artillery regiment. Napoleon's military career was set against a backdrop of significant global and local events. The American Revolution was unfolding, challenging the traditional power of monarchies and fueling democratic aspirations. At the same time in France, the Enlightenment was stirring public discontent with the absolute monarchy, setting the stage for the French Revolution. These events played a crucial role in shaping the era into which Napoleon stepped as he began his military journey. These were times of questioning established norms and pursuing modernization and rational governance. A time that would provide Bonaparte just the right chance to rise in ranks and cement his name in history.

---

1. The Age of Enlightenment, also known as the Age of Reason, was a cultural and intellectual movement in Europe that primarily spanned the 17th and 18th centuries. This era is characterized by a profound

emphasis on reason, individualism, and skepticism towards traditional doctrines and superstitions. Enlightenment thinkers advocated for scientific and intellectual inquiry, religious tolerance, and the idea that knowledge and education can lead to societal progress and reform.

TWO

The Path to Power: Ambition and Revolution (1785-1799)

In 1785, after becoming a lieutenant, Bonaparte divided his time between his military service and going back home to Corsica. His father's allegiance with Corsica had also taken its roots in Bonaparte and he showed deep interest in Corsician politics.

Soon after that, in 1788, Napoleon came back from Corsica and took up a place in an artillery school in Auxome. The backdrop of the revolution in France was heightening day by day and the year 1789 was a pivotal one for both Napoleon and France. The French Revolution began, radically altering the political and social landscape of the country. This period of upheaval and the ideals of the Revolution deeply influenced Napoleon. He closely followed the events in Paris, including the storming of the Bastille and the rise of revolutionary fervor across France. These occurrences resonated with his own Corsican experiences of resistance and rebellion against authority.

In the early years of the Revolution, Napoleon's career saw several ups and downs. He took leave from his military duties and returned to Corsica in 1789, where he became embroiled in complex local politics. His initial allegiance lay with Pasquale Paoli, the Corsican nationalist leader. However, ideological differences and political conflicts eventually led to a rupture between them. This conflict was emblematic of the larger tensions within the Revolution, between the goals of national unity and local autonomy.

During this time in Corsica, Napoleon also began to cultivate his skills as a political and military strategist. He was involved in several military engagements on the island, including an unsuccessful expedition to recapture Corsica's port city of Ajaccio from anti-revolutionary forces in 1793. These experiences provided him with invaluable insights into military tactics and leadership, further shaping his future military strategies.

By 1793, Napoleon had returned to France and was making his mark as an officer in the French army. His first major military success came with the Siege of Toulon, where he served as a captain of artillery. His expertise and strategic planning were instrumental in retaking the city from Royalist forces and their British allies. This victory earned him a promotion to Brigadier General at the young age of 24, marking the beginning of his rapid rise through the military ranks.

Yet, the political landscape in France was volatile during this period, marked by the Reign of Terror. In 1794, Napoleon was briefly detained for his association with the Robespierre brothers,[1] who had fallen from power. His arrest was short-lived, but this episode highlighted the precarious nature of the political environment.

After his release, Napoleon's career faced uncertainty. However, his fortunes changed in 1795. He was appointed to command the French army's artillery in Italy but did not take up this role immediately. Instead, he returned to Paris.

A significant turning point came on thirteen Vendémiaire, when Napoleon played a decisive role in  suppressing a Royalist uprising in Paris. Using a 'whiff of grapeshot,' as it became known, his actions saved the National Convention from the insurgents. This event greatly enhanced his reputation and put him in favor with the new government, the Directory.

Around this time, Napoleon also met Joséphine de Beauharnais, whom he would marry in March 1796. Joséphine, originally Marie Josèphe Rose Tascher de La Pagerie, entered Napoleon's life during a pivotal time in both their lives. Their social circles facilitated their meeting in Paris in 1795, intersecting at a time when France was still reeling from the Revolution. Joséphine, a prominent member of the Parisian social elite, had established herself in these circles through her first marriage to

Alexandre de Beauharnais, who was executed during the Reign of Terror.

Napoleon, then an ambitious and rising military officer, was immediately taken with Joséphine's grace and sophistication. Their first encounter was at a social event in Paris, where Joséphine's charm and wit captivated the young general. Despite the differences in their backgrounds, Joséphine being a part of the established social order and Napoleon still climbing the social ladder, their attraction was mutual and intense.

The courtship was swift, with Napoleon ardently pursuing Joséphine. Their relationship blossomed rapidly, fueled by Napoleon's fervent love letters, which have since become famous for their intensity and eloquence.

Their marriage in 1796 was not just a romantic union but also a strategic alliance for Napoleon. Joséphine's connections and status in French society gave him an entry into higher social circles, which were crucial for his political ambitions. On the other hand, Joséphine, a widow with two children and facing uncertain financial security, found stability and protection in her marriage to Napoleon, who was rapidly gaining prominence.

Before heading to Italy, Napoleon focused on reorganizing and revitalizing the army in the region, a task that required significant logistical and strategic planning. He worked tirelessly to prepare his troops, many of whom were demoralized and poorly equipped, for the upcoming campaign.

This could be considered Napoleon's first big break as he led the French army in Italy from 1796 to 1797 where he was appointed the commander in chief of the Alps Army. He took over an army that wasn't doing well and was facing a strong enemy in Austria. Napoleon brought new energy to his troops by fighting alongside them and promising them rewards for their victories. He changed the way his army fought, making them faster and more flexible, and used the element of surprise to beat the enemy.

He also had a hand in changing the political scene in Italy, making deals with the places he conquered, and sending back much-needed resources to the government in Paris. Napoleon's reputation as a military leader substantially increased after he won important battles like Lodi and Arcole, greatly boosting his standing in France with a total of eighteen victories during the Italian campaign.

After Italy, Napoleon wanted to take on bigger challenges. He looked to Egypt, hoping to disrupt British trade with India in 1798. Napoleon's army, consisting of around 35,000 soldiers, landed in Alexandria in July 1798. The French quickly captured the city and Napoleon moved his forces towards Cairo. The Battle of the Pyramids on July 21st, 1798, was a decisive victory for Napoleon.

The French forces secured a significant win by utilizing the infantry square[2] against the Mamluk cavalry. While a military success, the battle is also remembered for the scientific and cultural exploration it spurred, leading to the discovery of the Rosetta

Stone, which became crucial in deciphering Egyptian hieroglyphics.

Moreover, in Egypt, which was part of the Ottoman Empire but run by Mamluk Beys, Napoleon used other tactics like claiming he was the Ottoman's sultan's friend and wanted to reduce the Mamluks' power. He used religious messages to gain people's support. He started ruling the country by setting up councils and placing religious leaders (ulamas) in key positions in Cairo and other regions.

However, the naval Battle of the Nile, fought on August 1st, 1798, was a turning point in the campaign. The British Royal Navy, under Admiral Horatio Nelson, decimated the French fleet, leaving Napoleon's forces isolated in Egypt. This naval defeat was a significant setback, highlighting the strategic importance of naval power, which Napoleon notably lacked. The Egyptian Campaign continued with mixed results. While it achieved some military successes, it was hampered by issues such as disease, supply problems, and the challenge of guerilla warfare from local forces.

In 1801, with the French position in Egypt indefensible, the remnants of Napoleon's army surrendered to the British and Ottoman forces. In early 1799, Napoleon launched an invasion of Ottoman-ruled Syria, aiming to strike a further blow against British interests and perhaps even establish a French presence in the area. The campaign began successfully with the capture of towns like Gaza and Jaffa. However, the Siege of Acre, lasting from March to May 1799, was a significant setback. The city, defended by Ottoman and British forces, resisted repeated French assaults.

The failure at Acre, combined with the outbreak of plague among his troops, forced Napoleon to retreat to Egypt. The Syrian campaign exposed the logistical challenges of operating far from France and the limits of Napoleon's military reach.

Napoleon's Egyptian Campaign was not just a military endeavor but a remarkable journey of scientific and cultural discovery that significantly contributed to the Western understanding of ancient Egyptian civilization. When Napoleon embarked on this ambitious expedition to Egypt in 1798, he had brought along more than just soldiers; he was accompanied by a group of over 150 scholars and scientists. This team, known as the *Commission des Sciences et des Arts*, included engineers, botanists, artists, and historians. Their task was to study and document the ancient and modern aspects of Egyptian life.

One of the most significant contributions of this campaign was the discovery of the Rosetta Stone in July 1799 near  the town of Rosetta (Rashid).[3] This artifact, inscribed with the same text in three different scripts –Ancient Egyptian hieroglyphs, Demotic script, and Ancient Greek – was a key to deciphering Egyptian hieroglyphics. The study of the Rosetta Stone eventually enabled scholars to unlock the secrets of ancient Egyptian writing and literature, opening a new era in the field of Egyptology.

Furthermore, the scholars accompanying Napoleon conducted extensive surveys and excavations, which led to a deeper understanding of Egyptian history, culture, and architecture. Their findings were later published in the monumental work *Description de l'Égypte*, which provided Europeans with their first comprehensive study of Egyptian antiquities. This publication significantly influenced European art and architecture, sparking a wave of Egyptomania across the continent.

Napoleon's foray into Egypt was also notable for its attempts at cultural assimilation. He showed respect for local customs and religion, attempting to position himself as a liberator who would free the Egyptians from Mamluk rule. This approach, although met with mixed results, showcased Napoleon's understanding of the importance of cultural and religious sensitivity in governance.

In essence, the Egyptian campaign, while a mixed military venture, was a landmark in the history of cultural exchange and scientific exploration. It demonstrated Napoleon's appreciation for knowledge and culture and his ambition to extend French influence beyond mere territorial expansion. This campaign left a permanent mark on the study of ancient civilizations and exemplified the interconnectedness of military conquest and cultural enlightenment.

So, even though the campaigns in Italy and Egypt had different results, they were both important in showing Napoleon's leadership and strategist skills. They also showed some of his weaknesses, like taking on too much and not having a strong navy. Through all the disorder of the Revolution, Napoleon stood out not just as a general but as someone legendary. His big personality, success in battles, and smart political moves prepared him for his return to France and climb to the very top.

---

1. The Robespierre brothers, Maximilien and Augustin, were prominent figures during the French Revolution. Maximilien Robespierre (1758–1794) was the more famous of the two. He was a radical Jacobin leader and one of the principal figures in the French Revolution. Augustin Robespierre (1763–1794), the younger brother of Maximilien, was also actively involved in the revolutionary government.

2. The infantry square, also known as the square formation, is a military formation that was commonly used by infantry units in the 17th and 19th centuries, particularly effective against cavalry charges. This formation involves infantry soldiers standing in close order in a square, with soldiers on all sides facing outward.

3. The town of Rosetta, known in Arabic as Rashid, is a port city located in the Nile Delta in Egypt. It is famous for being the discovery site of the Rosetta Stone in 1799. The Rosetta Stone is a granodiorite stele inscribed with a decree issued in Memphis in 196 BC during the Ptolemaic dynasty.

THREE

Ascension of an Emperor: From Coup to Coronation (1799-1804)

As the 18th century was coming to an end, France was in turmoil, rocked by revolutionary fervor and political instability. In 1799, following mixed fortunes in Egypt, Napoleon returned to France. Despite setbacks in the Middle East, he was greeted as a hero, his reputation as a military genius intact. His success in Italy and his resolute leadership in Egypt had captured the public imagination, positioning him as a potential leader in the tumultuous French political landscape.

French politics at the time was a labyrinth of factions and power struggles. The government, known as the Directory, was weak and divided. Napoleon, with his military power and popularity, found himself at the center of these difficult times. Influential figures like Emmanuel Joseph Sieyès, a key member of the Directory, saw in Napoleon the military brightness needed to stabilize the government.

The year 1799 was pivotal. Sieyès and his ally Roger Ducos plotted a coup to overhaul the Directory. They needed a strong military leader and Napoleon was the obvious choice. In November 1799, known in the revolutionary calendar as Brumaire, the coup was executed. However, it encountered resistance, particularly in the Council of 500 where Napoleon was physically attacked. It was only with the intervention of his loyal soldiers that the coup succeeded, leading to the dissolution of the Directory.

In the aftereffects of the coup, a new regime was established — the Consulate, consisting of three consuls: Sieyès, Ducos, and Napoleon. Initially seen as the junior partner, Napoleon swiftly bypassed his colleagues, securing power in his hands. He became the First Consul, and effectively the de facto ruler of France. His ascent was marked by both his adeptness in navigating the political area and his ability to capitalize on the public's desire for stability and strong leadership.

As First Consul, Napoleon embarked on a series of reforms aimed at stabilizing and modernizing France. In 1800, he created the Banque de France to make the money system stable after the Revolution. This helped make sure the country had enough money and was financially stable.

He restructured the French government, implemented legal reforms such as the Napoleonic Code, and focused on rebuilding the French economy. He changed the country's laws, government, and economy. One of his biggest changes was the Napoleonic Code, or the Civil Code of the French, introduced in 1804. Before this, France had many different local laws and rules from kings or lords.

Jean-Jacques Régis de Cambacérès first tried to make a single set of laws, but only some of his ideas were used. When Napoleon became the leader in 1799, he got a group of top lawyers, led by Cambacérès, to finish the Code. They finished it in 1801, but it was only published in 1804.

The Napoleonic Code established a unified set of laws for all of France, drawing inspiration from French Revolution ideals such as the equality of all before the law and the protection of individuals' property. It got rid of old privileges based on birth, allowed freedom of religion, and made sure people could keep their property. But it also showed Napoleon's old-fashioned views on women by giving them fewer rights.

The Code's influence was far-reaching, spreading throughout Europe and beyond during the Napoleonic Wars. This Code changed laws all over Europe and even in the United States, in places like Louisiana. It ended feudalism and helped free people who were bound to the land in the areas where it was used. This was a big change from the old conflict between the king's power and the rights of different social classes. Now, the law was clear and easy for everyone to understand. His reign was characterized by a mix of strict rule and smart updates, aiming to keep the Revolution's successes while getting rid of its over-the-top aspects.

By the end of the 18th century, the Catholic Church in France had lost much of its old glory and influence, a direct consequence of the Revolution. Napoleon, recognizing the Church's power as a unifying force, saw an opportunity to use this for his own political ends. His way of doing this wasn't because he was devout or because he wanted to give the Church its old power back. Instead, it was a calculated move to stabilize his regime and gain widespread support.

Napoleon's main move came on July 15, 1801, with the signing of the agreement with Pope

Pius VII. This agreement recognized Catholicism as the main religion of most people in France, but it didn't make it the official state religion. This distinction was important as it allowed Napoleon to satisfy both the Church and the secular factions within France.

Napoleon's decision to reinstate the Church was met with mixed reactions. While this move upset some revolutionary groups, especially the Jacobins and extreme thinkers who saw it as going against the Revolution's dislike of the Church, it was admired by most people and immensely popular among the general population. For many, the restoration of Catholic practices and reopening of churches symbolized a return to normalcy and stability.

It's important to understand that Napoleon bringing back the Church was just a step towards a bigger goal. Under his rule, the Church didn't have the same old power. Instead, it was more like a part of the government that Napoleon controlled. He made sure the Church didn't get back the lands it lost during the Revolution, keeping the changes made by the Revolution.

This approach to the Church was part of a bigger plan. On February 7, 1800, a national vote asked the French if they wanted Napoleon as consul for life. The results on February 18 showed a substantial majority in favor, with over 3 million people voting 'Yes,' compared to just 1,562 who voted 'No.' This historical vote is believed by some to have been rigged by Bonaparte's brother in his favor. But, consequently of the vote, the rules were changed and Napoleon became "Consul for Life." This was a big step towards becoming Emperor. He started to make his power stronger, controlled the news, and stopped people from disagreeing with him. His success in battles also helped make him more powerful and respected.

He also used art to further his political agenda. Many artists also flourished under Napoleon's patronage. Alongside Jacques-Louis David, his support benefited artists like Antoine-Jean Gros, Jean-Auguste-Dominique Ingres, and Anne-Louis Girodet. Their works often depicted key events of the Napoleonic era. They contributed to the romanticized vision of Napoleon's military and political career by creating works like "The Coronation of Napoleon" and "Napoleon Crossing the Alps." Napoleon also used art as a diplomatic tool, gifting artworks to allies and important European figures. This practice not only demonstrated his appreciation for the arts but also served to extend his influence and cultivate favorable relations.

Napoleon was a patron of the arts and utilized them to glorify his regime and promote the ideals of the Empire. He understood  the power of art as a form of propaganda and used it to create his public image and immortalize his achievements. Artworks commissioned by him often depicted him as a larger-than-life figure, emphasizing his role as a military genius and a benevolent ruler. This approach helped shape public perception and reinforced his authority. Under Napoleon, Neoclassicism became the dominant artistic style he favored for its ability to convey the grandeur and timelessness associated with classical antiquity.

Thus after a long journey of establishing his image, on December 2, 1804, in a lavish ceremony at Notre Dame Cathedral in Paris, Napoleon crowned himself Emperor of the French, marking the climax of his rise from a military leader to the absolute ruler of France. The coronation, attended by Pope Pius VII, was a symbolic assertion of his authority and a break from the traditional monarchical power structures of Europe. The ceremony of Napoleon's coronation as Emperor of the French was a reminder of the greatness of the ancient pharaohs. The self-coronation was a bold statement, a reminder taking people back to his magnificent presence in Egypt. It symbolized his belief in his destined role and authority, asserting that his power stemmed from the people's support rather than any divine right or god-given power. Alongside him, Joséphine became the first Empress. Her coronation was a lavish affair, reflecting Napoleon's love for her and the importance of her position. As Empress, Joséphine played a vital role in the court's social life and was admired for her style and grace.

Napoleon, now Emperor Napoleon I, had not only secured his position at the helm of France but also had reshaped the French nation, leaving an unremovable mark on its history and that of Europe.

FOUR

The New Empire: Battles and Rule (1804/1805-1807)

1804 was a monumental year for France and for Napoleon Bonaparte. After years of political upheaval, the French Senate had declared Napoleon as Emperor on May 18th. As Emperor, Napoleon didn't just solidify his power; he embarked on a journey to reshape the European landscape.

The year 1805 was marked by significant military actions in the new Empire, the most notable being the Battle of Trafalgar and the Battle of Austerlitz. The Battle of Trafalgar, occurring on October 21st, was a naval confrontation where the British Royal Navy, under Admiral Nelson, dealt a crushing defeat to the combined fleets of France and Spain. This battle was a turning point in naval warfare, establishing British supremacy on the seas. For France, it exposed the weaknesses of their naval forces, which lacked England's rich tradition of naval power. Despite having formidable ships and competent commanders, the French Navy was hampered by insufficient supplies, poorly maintained ships, and a lack of experienced officers, many of whom had fled the country or joined the merchant marine.

On December 2nd, Napoleon achieved a resounding victory against Austria and Russia at the Battle of Austerlitz, also known as the Battle of the Three Emperors. This battle is often regarded as Napoleon's greatest victory, where his strategic brilliance outshined the combined forces of two great European powers.

Facing a combined Russo-Austrian force, Napoleon cleverly faked weakness to draw his enemies into a vulnerable position. Under the command of Tsar Alexander I of Russia[1] and Holy Roman Emperor Francis II, the allied armies over confident, stretched their lines thin, falling right into Napoleon's trap. With their superior mobility and cohesion, the French troops struck decisively and exploited the enemy's overextension, resulting in confusion among the Russo-Austrian forces. The battle resulted in approximately 36,000 Allied casualties compared to 9,000 French. The French captured 20,000 prisoners and 180 cannons.

The victory at Austerlitz was not just a display of military prowess but also had profound political repercussions. The win effectively dissolved the Third Coalition against France and solidified Napoleon's position as the dominant force in Central Europe. The triumph compelled Austria to sign the Treaty of Pressburg, surrendering significant territories to France and its allies and marking a high point in Napoleon's imperial reign. The battle not only demonstrated his military genius but also significantly enhanced his position in Europe, striking fear into the hearts of his enemies.

In 1806, Napoleon continued to expand his influence. On July 12th, he established the Confederation of the Rhine, a collection of German states under French protection, effectively dissolving the Holy Roman Empire. This move was a strategic effort to consolidate his power in Germany and to create a buffer zone against his enemies.

The military campaign of 1806 culminated in the Battle of Jena-Auerstedt on October 14th. The Prussian army was soundly defeated by Napoleon's forces. At Jena, Napoleon himself directed the French forces against Prince Hohenlohe's Prussian army. Simultaneously, at Auerstedt, Marshal Davout faced a larger Prussian force under the command of the Duke of Brunswick. Both battles demonstrated the effectiveness of Napoleon's modern tactics against the outdated Prussian military doctrine. The Prussian Army suffered around 25,000 casualties in the aftermath, while French losses were about 14,000.

The French forces, utilizing rapid operations and coordinated attacks, overwhelmed the Prussian armies on both fronts. The aftermath was devastating for Prussia: the French captured Berlin and the military collapse led to significant territorial losses in the Treaty of Tilsit. The defeat at Jena-Auerstedt also marked the beginning of Prussia's reform of its military. Overall, these battles marked the fall of Prussia as a major European power and showcased Napoleon's army's strategic agility and operational efficiency. This victory was not just a triumph on the battlefield; it marked the decline of Prussia as a significant military power and expanded Napoleon's control over much of Germany.

Perhaps the most significant non-military event of 1806 was the establishment of the Continental System, initiated by the Berlin Decree on November 21st. This was an economic blockade against Britain, designed to destroy its economy by cutting off its trade with Europe. However, the system proved difficult to enforce and had unintended consequences. It led to widespread economic hardship across Europe, including in France, and spurred smuggling and illegal trade. The blockade aimed to weaken Britain but ended up straining the economies of a lot of the continental nations.

One of his other important non-military contributions in this stage to reshape France was to expand and reorganize the Louvre Museum. He enriched its collections with artworks seized during his military campaigns across Europe, turning it into one of the world's greatest art repositories.

In 1807, Napoleon's attention turned to the Iberian Peninsula. On May 2nd, he began the Peninsular War, a costly and prolonged conflict in Spain. His decision to invade Spain and Portugal was driven partly by their alliance with England and partly by his desire to enforce the Continental System. However, the campaign in Spain exposed the limitations of Napoleon's military strategy and his underestimation of guerrilla warfare[2] that was led under Duke Wellington.

The installation of his brother, Joseph Bonaparte, as King of Spain on July 20th was also met with fierce resistance from the Spanish population. The Peninsular War drained French resources, stretched its military thin, and, ultimately, became one of Napoleon's most significant miscalculations. The rugged terrain of Spain, the hostility of the populace, and the challenges in maintaining supply lines turned the campaign into a quagmire for French forces.

1. Tsar Alexander I of Russia (1777–1825) was the Emperor of Russia from 1801 to 1825 and is often remembered for his role in the Napoleonic Wars and for his efforts in European diplomacy. Ascending to the throne after the assassination of his father, Tsar Paul I, Alexander's reign marked a period of significant political and social change in Russia.

2. Guerrilla warfare is a form of irregular warfare in which small groups of combatants, such as paramilitary personnel, armed civilians, or irregulars, use military tactics including ambushes, sabotage, raids, petty warfare, hit-and-run tactics, and mobility to fight a larger and less-mobile traditional military. It is a type of warfare characterized by its reliance on the element of surprise, deep knowledge of the terrain, and the support of the local population.

FIVE

Personal and Professional Life: Turmoils and Transition (1808-1810)

The year 1808 marked a significant shift in Napoleon Bonaparte's reign. The move of installing his brother on the Spanish throne was seen as an assertion of the Bonaparte dynasty's influence, which was met with widespread opposition by the people and had significant repercussions. Moreover, this decision also strained Napoleon's relationship with his brother, who found the Spanish crown a burdensome and precarious position.

In 1809 things took a turn again; the Austrian Empire, reinvigorated and seeking to avenge previous defeats, challenged Napoleon. The Battle of Wagram in July was particularly noteworthy. While it ended in a French victory, it was a hard-fought and costly battle, indicating a resurgence in Austrian military prowess. Napoleon's forces, even though triumphant, were stretched increasingly thin, and had to battle on multiple fronts to win the war.

This year also brought personal turmoil for Napoleon. The Empress Josephine, who had long been a companion and confidante, was unable to provide an heir, leading to the dissolution of their marriage. This was also heightened by rumors of infidelity on Josephine's part. The decision to end the marriage was not merely personal but deeply political, reflecting Napoleon's desire to secure his legacy and strengthen alliances through marriage.

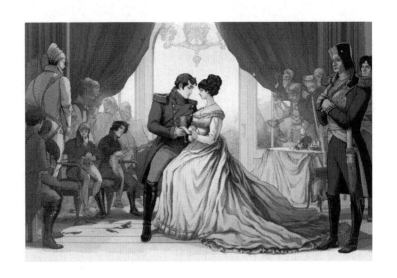

Thus, In 1810, Napoleon's personal life took a dramatic turn with his marriage to Marie Louise, the daughter of the Emperor of Austria. This marriage was more than a personal union; it was a significant political alliance between former enemies. Marie Louise, the niece of Marie Antoinette, represented a bridge between France and one of its most formidable adversaries, Austria.

Marie Louise adapted to her role as Empress, though she initially found the transition challenging, given the political backdrop and the large shoes of Joséphine to fill. However, her primary role in Napoleon's life was to produce an heir.

Amidst the personal changes, Napoleon continued to implement significant domestic reforms in France and the territories under his control. However, his Continental System which he strengthened and reinforced, and which was intended to weaken Britain economically, was facing challenges. The blockade was difficult to enforce and was causing economic strain in France and its allies, leading to increasing discontent among European nations. Moreover, as a part of restructuring the German territories, Napoleon created the Grand Duchy of Frankfurt, a puppet state under French influence.

By 1810, Napoleon's leadership style had evolved. The charismatic leader, once known for his close involvement with his troops and bold military strategies, was increasingly seen as distant and autocratic. His relentless pursuit of power and territorial expansion led to growing dissent within the French military and government, and restlessness among the French populace.

The years from 1808 to 1810 marked a period of contrast and complexity in Napoleon's life. They were marked by significant military engagements, a major personal and political transition through his marriage to Marie Louise, and the ongoing challenges of ruling a vast and diverse empire. These years laid the groundwork for the later stages of his reign, characterized by heightened European conflicts, internal dissent, and the eventual decline of the Napoleonic Empire.

SIX

The Russian Campaigns: The Begin of the Fall (1810-1813)

In 1810, Napoleon Bonaparte, Emperor of the French, despite the recent challenges in his personal and professional life, was at the height of his power. His empire stretched from Spain to Russia, commanding the respect and fear of

Europe. Soon, in 1811, his goal to have an heir was also achieved with the birth of his son with Marie Louise, Napoleon François Joseph Charles Bonaparte, known as the King of Rome. This birth was celebrated throughout the Empire, as it secured the succession of the Bonaparte dynasty.

By this time, Napoleon had also changed how France was divided up. He got rid of the old system based on history or feudalism and made a new system with departments that were about the same size and had the same number of people. By 1812, France had over 130 departments.

Each department had a leader called a prefect, picked by Napoleon for their loyalty and skill, not local connections. These prefects made sure the government's laws and policies were followed, collected taxes, managed the police, and looked after public projects. There were also sub-prefects and mayors who helped run smaller areas. This made the government more central and reduced the power of local nobles and regional authorities.

The tax system was also changed to be fairer and work better. Napoleon introduced a direct tax system that was easier on the poor and brought in more money for the government. This included taxes on land, people, windows and doors, and luxury items. The tax system was simpler and fairer, fitting with the Revolution's ideas of equality. Napoleon also made sure properties were accurately measured so taxes could be fair.

But, the Peninsular War (1807–1814) that had started in 1807 was increasingly becoming a thorn in Napoleon's side.  His decision to place his brother Joseph on the Spanish throne had sparked a widespread resistance, leading to a guerilla war. The Battle of Bussaco in Portugal, where the French suffered a setback, highlighted the challenges Napoleon faced in maintaining his dominance. As Masséna, the person appointed by Bonaparte for the battle, advanced into Portugal, Wellington (the leader of the other army) retreated to draw the French into a more favorable position for the allied forces. Wellington chose to make a stand at the Serra do Buçaco, a mountain ridge in central Portugal. The place provided a significant advantage to the defending forces, offering high ground and natural barriers against attackers. Masséna launched a frontal assault on the allied position. Despite facing a huge and well-formed enemy, the French were confident, relying on their numerical superiority and the prowess of their troops.

The battle was fierce, with French forces repeatedly trying to scale the heights of the ridge. However, they were met with intense resistance from the Anglo-Portuguese troops, who were well-prepared and positioned. The French suffered heavy casualties as they attempted to climb the steep slopes under constant fire. Wellington had deployed his troops effectively, utilizing the natural defenses of the ridge. The British and Portuguese soldiers, many of whom were veterans of previous campaigns, fought tenaciously, repelling the French assaults. By the end of the day, the French had failed to break through Wellington's lines and suffered significant losses. Masséna realized that a frontal assault was not working and decided to withdraw. The Battle of Bussaco was a clear victory for Wellington and his forces, demonstrating their ability to hold their ground against the seasoned French army.

Despite the battle, this conflict continued and it is often referred to as the "Spanish Ulcer," as it reduced French military strength and exposed the vulnerabilities of Napoleon's empire. The term "Spanish Ulcer" was given by Napoleon himself, expressing his frustration with the prolonged and costly nature of the war in the

Iberian Peninsula, as this war diverted attention and resources from other fronts, contributing to the eventual weakening of Napoleon's hold over Europe.

Despite facing losses in the Spanish Ulcer, Napoleon's desire to rule the world was still high. In 1812, he made a fateful decision to invade Russia. Napoleon's Russian Campaign, often seen as one of the biggest military mistakes in history, was a key moment in his reign. He wanted to force Tsar Alexander I of Russia to stick to the Continental System, a blockade against Britain, and keep French power strong in Europe.

 In June 1812, Napoleon led a huge army, more than 600,000 soldiers, into Russia. This Grande Armée included troops from various parts of Napoleon's European empire. Initially, they moved quickly through Russia gaining some success, but the Russian army avoided big battles and retreated, burning lands and villages to stop the French from finding food and shelter.

A critical moment was when Napoleon took Moscow in September 1812. The Russians didn't surrender and Moscow was set on fire, leaving the French without needed resources.

The Russian winter soon began, with extremely cold temperatures. The French army, not prepared for this cold and lacking food, started a disastrous retreat.

The retreat was a nightmare. The soldiers faced freezing cold, hunger, diseases, and attacks by Russian forces. Many died, and by the time Napoleon got back to France in December, only a small part of his army was left. This campaign was a huge failure, weakening Napoleon's forces and encouraging his enemies in Europe.

After the terrible retreat from Moscow, Napoleon faced the Battle of Leipzig, fought from October 16 to 19, 1813. This battle involved many European countries, making it one of the largest and bloodiest of the Napoleonic Wars.

Following the Russian Campaign, a coalition of Russia, Prussia, Austria, and Sweden formed against Napoleon. Their armies met Napoleon's in Leipzig, Saxony. Napoleon, though outnumbered, decided to fight.

The battle was enormous, with over 600,000 soldiers. It included massive artillery fire, cavalry charges, and intense fighting. Napoleon fought hard, showing his skills in handling such a large battle. However, the coalition forces, well-coordinated, slowly pushed back the French.

A key moment was when Swedish-led forces, commanded by Napoleon's former marshal Jean-Baptiste Bernadotte, attacked the French. The Saxons, who had been fighting for the French, also switched sides, helping the coalition.

After four days, Napoleon ordered a retreat. A bridge's early destruction during the retreat led to many French losses. This battle was a big defeat for Napoleon, forcing French troops out of Germany and weakening his control in Europe.

In these times of bloodshed and war, the silver lining was that these Napoleonic "Wars" had provided a  propelling force for scientific and medical advancements. The need for better ways to treat wounded soldiers on the battlefield led to improvements in surgical techniques and medical care. Thus, showing Napoleon's influence beyond the battlefield.

SEVEN

The Turning Tide: From Moscow to Elba (1813-1815)

The seeds of Napoleon's fall were sown with his ill-fated Russian campaign in 1812. After losing at Leipzig, Napoleon's empire started to fall apart. By March 1814, the coalition forces had taken over Paris. Napoleon's rule in France was no longer possible. So, on April 6th, 1814, he had to give up his throne. The Treaty of Fontainebleau was signed, marking the end of his time as Emperor of the French. This treaty sent him to exile on Elba, a small island near Italy. He was given control over the island, but it was more like keeping him under watch.

Napoleon's time in Elba, from April 1814 to February 1815, wasn't just a fall from power. Upon arrival in Elba, Napoleon, though stripped of his vast empire, did not lose his passion for administration and reform. He took charge of this small island with a population of about 12,000, and started acting as a mini-sovereign. He began organizing Elba's defenses and established a small but symbolic navy.

He also focused on improving Elba's economy. He initiated the development of the island's iron mines in Rio

Marina. He introduced modern agricultural techniques and crop rotation, which improved local farming. He also embarked on infrastructure projects, improving the road

network to facilitate easier movement across the island. In Portoferraio, the island's capital, Bonaparte initiated urban planning and beautification projects. He had streets repaired and public buildings renovated, and aimed to turn Portoferraio into a model city.

Despite all the work, while in Elba, Napoleon often felt isolated and was deeply affected by the absence of his wife, Marie Louise, and his son. Despite his repeated requests, they did not join him in Elba. He maintained correspondence with his mother, Letizia Ramolino, and his sister, Princess Pauline Bonaparte, who occasionally visited him. Given the free time, there was also a mix of reflective introspection and restless planning. Napoleon often pondered over his past decisions, particularly the failed Russian campaign, and contemplated his future. Despite the outward appearance of a ruler content with his dominion, he was internally brewing plans for a return to power.

With the help of loyalists who visited him, Napoleon kept a keen eye on the political situation in Europe. He was particularly interested in the Congress of Vienna, where the fate of the nations he once ruled was being decided. Reports of growing discontent with the Bourbon restoration in France reached him, fueling his desire for a comeback.

Taking up the opportunity, Napoleon used his time in Elba to carefully plan his escape. He maintained secret communication with his supporters in France, assessing the mood of the military and the public. Despite the small size of his forces in Elba, Napoleon worked to ensure their loyalty and readiness. He regularly drilled his troops, composed of a few hundred men, to maintain military discipline and preparedness.

In February 1815, after almost a year in Elba, Napoleon saw his opportunity. He had observed the European powers' focus on the Congress of Vienna and sensed the unrest in France against

King Louis XVIII's regime. With a small band of loyal soldiers, he embarked on the ship Inconstant and made his daring escape, marking the beginning of the Hundred Days and his brief return to power in France.

EIGHT

Hundred Days and Waterloo: The Last Stand (1815-1840)

Napoleon's escape from Elba in February 1815 and his subsequent return to France marked the beginning of a remarkable period in history, known as the Hundred Days. He landed in France on March 1st, 1815, and quickly began rallying support. His journey from the south of France to Paris was a strategic win. As he continued his journey, many soldiers, discomforted with the Bourbon monarchy, switched their allegiance to him. By the time he reached Paris in late March, his force had grown significantly, leading to King Louis XVIII's quick departure.

During this renewed but brief reign, Napoleon worked tirelessly. His focus was on reforming the administration and rebuilding the French army. He aimed to reassure the European powers, particularly those gathered at the Congress of Vienna, of his peaceful intentions. However, his return to power alarmed these nations, who quickly labeled him an outlaw and prepared to unite against him once more.

Napoleon introduced several reforms to address issues from his previous reign. He proposed a new, more liberal constitution, hoping to gain public support amid the growing tensions. However, this era was overshadowed by the looming threat of war, requiring him to dedicate significant resources to military preparation.

The climax of Napoleon's Hundred Days came at the Battle of Waterloo on June 18, 1815. The battle, near Brussels, Belgium, saw Napoleon facing off against a British-led coalition under the Duke of Wellington, complemented by Prussian forces which were led by Gebhard Leberecht von Blücher.

The battle began with an offensive[1] by Napoleon against the British forces. Initially, the French army found success, pushing back Wellington's troops. However, the situation dramatically shifted with the arrival of Blücher's Prussian forces. Wellington's disciplined defense, combined with the Prussian attack on Napoleon's flank, decisively turned the battle against the French. This resulted in a catastrophic defeat for Napoleon, sealing the fate of his empire.

After the devastating defeat at Waterloo, Napoleon returned to Paris, where he encountered strong political resistance and a lack of military options. Realizing the futility of his position, he abdicated for the second time on June 22nd, 1815. His initial plan was to seek refuge in the United States, but with British naval forces blocking the French coast, this became impossible. Ultimately, he surrendered to the British and was exiled to the remote island of Saint Helena in the South Atlantic.

Napoleon arrived at Saint Helena in October 1815, after a lengthy and challenging sea trip. His residence, Longwood House, was a modest, damp dwelling, far removed from the grand and majestic housing he once knew. Despite these humble conditions, Napoleon maintained a sense of dignity and routine, surrounded by a small group of loyal followers, including General Henri Bertrand and Count Charles de Montholon.

His time on Saint Helena was spent engaging in various activities. He dictated memoirs, reflecting on his life and campaigns, read extensively, and even started gardening. He often engaged in conversations with the British governor and other visitors, striving to influence his legacy and historical narrative.

The British, led by Governor Sir Hudson Lowe, imposed strict restrictions on Napoleon, limiting his communication and movement. These conditions, coupled with his isolation and limited contact with his family in Europe, contributed to a sense of loneliness and frustration.

Napoleon's health gradually declined during his exile. He suffered from various ailments, with his condition worsening due to the island's damp climate. His declining health and the hardships of his exile marked a stark contrast to his former power and influence.

Napoleon Bonaparte passed away in Saint Helena, at the age of 51. In 1840, his remains were returned to France and interred at Les Invalides in Paris, where they remain a site of remembrance and reflection on his tumultuous life and impact on history.

---

1. In military terms, an "offensive" refers to a coordinated military action or campaign primarily aimed at aggressively attacking and engaging an adversary with the objective of defeating them, capturing territory, or causing significant damage to their forces. It is characterized by proactive and assertive maneuvers as opposed to defensive tactics, which focus on protecting and holding one's own position. An offensive can take various forms, including a full-scale invasion, a targeted strike, or a series of coordinated attacks.

NINE

Veiled in Mystery: the Enigma of Napoleon's Demise

The famous historical figure died on May 5th, 1821, on Saint Helena, a remote island. Like Napoleon's life, his death has been a topic of much discussion and mystery, sparking various theories that still interest many people.

While living in exile on Saint Helena, Napoleon's health got worse. He often had stomach pain and other health problems. In the time leading up to his death, these health issues became more severe, and he spent a lot of time in bed at Longwood House, where he lived.

After Napoleon died, his personal doctor, Dr. Francesco Antommarchi, and some British doctors did an autopsy. They said he died of stomach cancer, a disease that also killed his father. For a long time, most people believed this explanation.

However, in the 1960s, a new idea came up. Tests on Napoleon's hair showed he had a lot of arsenic in his body. This finding led some to think he might have been poisoned, maybe even by the British who were watching over him.

However, later studies and a better understanding of that time period provided alternative explanations for the presence of arsenic. In that era, arsenic was found in items such as wallpaper and medicines. This suggests that Napoleon might have been exposed to arsenic frequently, not necessarily poisoned intentionally.

Today, experts still debate how Napoleon died. Some think the original idea of stomach cancer makes sense because of his symptoms and family history. Others can't ignore the high arsenic levels in his hair, which might point to being exposed to arsenic over a long time, maybe without anyone meaning to poison him.

Napoleon's death, like his life, is full of facts and stories that are hard to separate. The questions and theories about how he died make his life story even more interesting. His death marked the end of an important time in history, but his story continues to be fascinating and important.

Overall, the mystery of Napoleon's death adds to his legend. Whether he died from cancer, arsenic, or something else, he remains a significant historical figure whose life and death are still talked about and studied today.

TEN

The Lasting Legacy: Continued Influence after Death

Napoleon Bonaparte, a name that has evoked images of grandeur, military genius, and imperial power, has surpassed the bounds of time to become an almost mythic presence. The 'Napoleonic Myth' is an idea that adds to it. It is a varied and evolving phenomenon, containing a variety of narratives and interpretations that have been built around his life and legacy.

The Napoleonic Myth began to take shape following Napoleon's death in 1821. The story of his life, a young Corsican rising to become the Emperor of France, captured the public imagination. His military campaigns, which reshaped the map of Europe, and his administrative reforms, particularly the Napoleonic Code, added layers of complexity to his story.

Central to the Napoleonic Myth is the portrayal of Napoleon as a Romantic hero. His rise from modest and middle-class beginnings, marked by a combination of ambition, intellect, and charisma, fits the archetype of a self-made man defying the odds. His military strategies and victories, especially in battles like Austerlitz, are often highlighted as evidence of his genius. This aspect of the myth focuses on his achievements and often shadows the cost of his wars that resulted in many deaths and instability.

However, the Napoleonic Myth is not without its controversies. Napoleon's role in reinstating slavery in French colonies, after it had been abolished, is a stark reminder of the contradictions in his policies. Furthermore, the wars he led resulted in immense loss of life and widespread devastation, raising questions about the cost of his ambitions. These aspects contribute to a more nuanced and sometimes critical view of his legacy.

Napoleon's impact extends beyond historical and political realms into cultural representation. His image, with the famous hand-in-coat pose, has been immortalized in paintings, literature, and pop culture. The symbolic power of his figure has been used in various artistic expressions, contributing to the enduring nature of the myth.

Politically, Napoleon's image has been used to represent a range of ideologies. For some, he is a symbol of tyranny and military aggression, while for others, he represents a visionary leader who brought about much-needed reforms. The flexibility of his image allows for varied interpretations, depending on the viewer's perspective.

In France, Napoleon is celebrated as a national icon who brought glory to the nation and solidified its status as a major European power. His reign is often seen as a period of significant reforms that modernized France, with the Napoleonic Code being a particularly notable legacy. This code reformed French legal systems and continues to influence legal frameworks in many countries.

In contemporary times, the Napoleonic Myth continues to evolve. It serves as a subject of academic study and popular interest, with debates about his role in history being as lively today as they were centuries ago. The fascination with Napoleon speaks to the complexity of his character and the impact of his actions, which continue to provoke discussion and analysis. Napoleon's story is not merely a tale of a historical figure but a narrative woven into the fabric of human history and culture, continuing to captivate and intrigue.

The enduring legacy of Napoleon Bonaparte stretches well beyond France's borders, leaving an unremovable mark on the world stage. His legacy is not confined to his military conquests and political reforms within France but extends globally, influencing various aspects of modern governance, law, and military strategy.

Napoleon's impact was felt across Europe and beyond during his reign and continues to be significant. His military campaigns not only reshaped European geopolitics but also introduced new concepts in warfare and strategy that influenced military thinking worldwide.

The Napoleonic Code, perhaps his most enduring legacy, has had a lasting impact on legal systems around the world. Its principles of equality before the law, freedom of religion, and the sanctity of private property have been adopted in various forms in numerous countries.

Countries like Italy and Germany experienced significant changes due to Napoleon's conquests and reforms. In Italy, his rule helped pave the way for the unification movement. In Germany, the dissolution of the Holy Roman Empire and subsequent reorganization of states contributed to the later unification of Germany.

Napoleon's military tactics and strategies, such as the corps system and his approach to artillery, influenced the development of modern military doctrine. His campaigns are studied in military academies worldwide for their strategic brilliance and innovation. The profound influence of Napoleon's military innovations is a clear testament to his enduring legacy, which is marked by both admiration for his tactical genius and a critical reassessment of his broader historical impact.

Napoleon's legacy in modern times is characterized by a duality that reflects the complexity of his actions and impact. He is often seen as a carrier of Enlightenment ideals, spreading concepts of secular governance, legal equality, and meritocracy. His reforms, particularly in the legal domain, laid the foundations for modern state systems in Europe and beyond. However, conversely, Napoleon is also viewed as a tyrant who plunged Europe into years of war, causing immense suffering and loss of life. His ambition and relentless pursuit of power are often criticized for their devastating impact on Europe.

But no matter the view, there is no denying that the Napoleonic Wars changed the face of warfare and profoundly affected European society. They led to significant loss of life and economic hardship, altering Europe's demographic and social landscape. The redrawing of boundaries and reshaping of political entities during his reign had long-lasting effects on European politics and international relations.

Napoleon's influence on global affairs and modern governance systems is undeniable, as is the controversy surrounding his methods and motives. In contemporary perspectives, Napoleon emerges as a dual figure; both a visionary who brought significant changes to the world and a controversial leader whose actions led to widespread conflict and suffering.

His influence is also seen in popular culture in many ways. From literature and film to art and the digital age, Napoleon's persona has been both celebrated and studied, illustrating his lasting influence on global culture.

Napoleon's life and reign have been a rich source of inspiration for writers and novelists over the centuries. He appears in Leo Tolstoy's epic novel "War and Peace," which portrays him as a significant historical figure whose actions set the backdrop for the story's events. In "Les Misérables" by Victor Hugo, Napoleon's influence on French society and politics forms a crucial context for the novel's plot and characters.

Beyond these classics, many books, both fiction and non-fiction, have been written about

Napoleon, exploring his military campaigns, his political strategies, and his personal life. These literary works range from biographies to historical novels, each offering different perspectives on his complex character.

Napoleon's association with the arts began during his reign, with artists like Jacques-Louis David creating iconic paintings that glorify his rule and victories. This tradition has continued, with countless artists depicting Napoleon in various forms over the years. These artworks range from heroic portrayals to more introspective and critical examinations of his life and impact.

The film industry has also long been fascinated with Napoleon. Movies like "Waterloo" (1970), "Napoleon" (1927), "The Emperor of Paris" (2018), and "Napoleon" (2023) depict different phases of his life, from his military campaigns to his personal struggles. These films often highlight his strategic mind and leadership qualities while delving into his character's more human aspects. In addition to biographical films, Napoleon often appears as a character in movies set during the Napoleonic era, underlining the extent to which his presence loomed over the 19th century.

Napoleon's legacy continues to capture the imagination in the modern digital age. He is featured in video games and online content, often focusing on his military tactics and battles. Strategy games like the "Total War" series allow players to emulate Napoleon's campaigns, bringing his military genius to a new generation.

In addition to his presence in video games, Napoleon's legacy has also found a unique place in the world of social media, particularly on platforms like Instagram and in the world of Internet memes. Here, he is often depicted with a blend of humor and admiration, becoming a symbol that resonates with a wide audience. On Instagram, accounts dedicated to historical content frequently feature images of Napoleon, accompanied by anecdotes or quotes, showcasing different phases of his personality, leadership, and military tactics.

In the world of memes, Napoleon is often employed as a symbol of ambition, strategy, and sometimes, the alienation and loneliness that comes with overreach and failure. The meme culture using Napoleon reflects how his image has been adapted to fit modern cultural expressions, turning him into an exemplary figure that transcends the traditional boundaries of historical discourse. His image and name are frequently referenced in music, television, and even advertising, demonstrating his status as a cultural icon.

As perspectives on history evolve, so too do interpretations of Bonaparte's legacy. Recent cultural depictions have begun to explore the more controversial aspects of his reign, such as his reinstatement of slavery in the French colonies and the cost of his wars. These reinterpretations offer a more nuanced view of his impact and legacy.

Napoleon Bonaparte's presence in popular culture is as diverse as the man himself. From glorified depictions of his military prowess to critical examinations of his political and personal life, his legacy continues to be a source of fascination and debate. The portrayal of Napoleon in literature, film, art, and digital media reflects his historical significance and underscores his enduring influence as a cultural icon. This universal presence in popular culture ensures that Napoleon's story remains relevant, engaging new audiences and prompting fresh perspectives on his complex legacy.

Conclusion

Reflecting on Napoleon Bonaparte's life and legacy takes us through a vast journey of human experiences. He rose from humble beginnings in Corsica to rule a vast European empire, showcasing both brilliance and overreach. His story is more than just history; it's a lesson on leadership, ambition, governance, and the impacts of power.

Napoleon's military brilliance shone in battles like Austerlitz and Jena-Auerstedt. He was a master of strategy, but his campaigns also had heavy costs. His disastrous Russian campaign and struggles in the Peninsular War are reminders of war's brutal reality.

Beyond war, Napoleon brought significant reforms. The Napoleonic Code, for example, reformed laws in France and influenced legal systems worldwide. His restructuring of French administration and policies like the Continental System aimed to modernize and control, leaving a lasting impact beyond France.

Napoleon's personal life was as complex as his public one. His relationships with Joséphine and Marie Louise, his family dynamics, and his quest for an heir show a man caught in the web of personal and political challenges.

His later years marked a dramatic shift. From his exile to Elba to his return during the Hundred Days and ultimate defeat at Waterloo, Napoleon's story turned from power to downfall. His lonely end on Saint Helena highlights the transient nature of power.

Since his death, Napoleon has become a symbol and a myth, a subject of endless debate and portrayal. From Tolstoy's writings to modern memes, he continues to captivate us. He's seen as a strategic genius, a ruler with enlightened ideas, and sometimes a cautionary tale of pride.

Napoleon's story is one of human effort, ambition, and leadership, intertwined with history's changing course. He was both a product and a creator of his time, leaving a legacy that resonates in modern governance, law, culture, and our collective consciousness. Studying Napoleon helps us understand the past and gain insights into the present and future, exploring the unending interplay of power, ambition, and the human condition. His life and legacy are a profound reminder of the heights of success and the depths of fall that can be experienced in a lifetime, shaping our understanding of history and its influential figures.

Bonus

LITTLE-KNOWN RANDOM FACTS ABOUT NAPOLEON

In the vast tapestry of history, Napoleon Bonaparte's monumental achievements often overshadow the lesser-known, yet equally fascinating, facets of his life. In this chapter, we peel back the layers of the familiar narrative to unveil random and intriguing facts as well as obscured details that offer a more nuanced perspective on the legendary leader.

• While often depicted as short, Napoleon's height was actually around 5 feet 6 inches (1.68 meters), which was average for a Frenchman of that era. The idea of him being very short may have originated from confusion with his Imperial Guard, which included taller soldiers.

• In contrast to conventional sleep patterns, Napoleon adopted a unique approach known as polyphasic sleep. Instead of having a single, extended sleep period, he took short naps throughout the day, maximizing his wakefulness and productivity.

• Napoleon Bonaparte was known for his distinctive daily bathing routine, during which he immersed himself in Eau de Cologne. It was believed that this practice not only helped him maintain personal hygiene but also had perceived health benefits.

• The French emperor had a specific preference for Jean Maria Farina Eau de Cologne, a renowned brand that originated in Germany. This choice reflected his attention to personal grooming and his appreciation for luxury goods.

• A testament to his intellectual prowess, Napoleon demonstrated a strong interest in mathematics, particularly excelling in geometry during his formative years at military school. This proficiency in mathematical principles later played a crucial role in his military strategies.

• Napoleon's grasp of geography was not merely utilitarian for military purposes; it extended to a genuine passion for cartography. His collection of maps was extensive, reflecting a deep understanding of the geographical landscapes that played a pivotal role in his military campaigns.

• Beyond his military campaigns, Napoleon was an avid chess player, demonstrating an astute understanding of strategic thinking. He often applied military strategy principles to the game, showcasing the interconnectedness of his intellectual pursuits.

• Despite his reputation as a military leader, Napoleon had a softer side, harboring a love for poetry. He found particular resonance in the works of French poet Jean Racine, appreciating the artistry and emotion conveyed through verse.

• Amidst his military and political responsibilities, Napoleon found solace and enjoyment in the world of opera. His appreciation for the works of Christoph Willibald Gluck underscored a more culturally refined aspect of his personality.

• Contrary to the image of a stern military leader, Napoleon harbored a passion for the works of William Shakespeare. Quoting from the renowned playwright, he revealed an affinity for the depth and complexity of human emotions portrayed in Shakespearean dramas.

• Amidst the complexities of ruling an empire, Napoleon retained a fondness for a simple pleasure – rice pudding. This culinary preference hinted at a more down-to-earth aspect of his tastes.

• Napoleon's iconic bicorne hat not only became a symbol of his authority but also influenced fashion trends of the time. The distinctive way in which he wore the hat gave rise to the "Napoleon hat" style, showcasing his impact on cultural aesthetics.

• The emperor acquired various nicknames throughout his life, each contributing to the multifaceted image of the man. From the endearing "Little Corporal" (Le Petit Caporal) to the menacing "Corsican Ogre," these monikers added layers to his persona.

• Napoleon was proficient in multiple languages. He was not only a native French speaker but also spoke Italian and Corsican fluently. Additionally, he had a working knowledge of English and German.

• Napoleon and his first wife, Josephine, maintained a passionate and extensive correspondence throughout their relationship. Over 1,100 letters exchanged between them have been preserved, revealing the depth of their emotions and the challenges they faced.

• Preserved at the Army Museum in Paris, the bloodstained flag from the Battle of Marengo served as a tangible relic of Napoleon's military exploits. Carried by the emperor himself, it symbolized both triumph and sacrifice.

• Napoleon's personal seal, featuring an eagle, became an emblem associated with his reign. The symbolic choice of an eagle reflected the strength, power, and imperial aspirations of his regime.

• Napoleon was known for his love of animals, especially dogs. He had several canine companions, and during his exile on Saint Helena, he formed a close bond with a dog named Patras, which became his loyal companion.

• One of the more enigmatic aspects of Napoleon's personal life was his fear of cats. Whether rooted in a childhood incident or a deeper psychological layer, this fear added a touch of vulnerability to the formidable leader.

• Napoleon's favorite horse was Marengo, named after the Battle of Marengo, one of his significant victories. Marengo was an Arab stallion and became Napoleon's loyal companion in many battles. The horse was grey and became quite famous, being immortalized in several paintings depicting Napoleon. Marengo carried Napoleon in battles such as Austerlitz, Jena, Wagram, and Waterloo. After Napoleon's defeat at Waterloo in 1815, Marengo was captured by the British. The horse lived out the remainder of its days in England and died in 1831. Today, Marengo's skeleton is on display at the National Army Museum in London.

References

Avrom, David. *Napoleon: A Concise Biography*. Oxford: Oxford University Press, 2015.

Bayford, Katherine. *Napoleon: the revolutionary who made himself an emperor*. Engelsberg Ideas (2023). https://engelsbergideas.com/reviews/napoleon-the-revolutionary-who-made-himself-an-emperor/. Accessed Dec 20, 2023.

Clinger, James. *Napoleon Bonaparte, the French Revolution, and America's Protection of the Newly Formed United States Against Tyranny*. Constituting America (2022). https://constitutingamerica.org/90day-aer-napoleon-bonaparte-the-french-revolution-and-americas-protection-of-the-newly-formed-united-states-against-tyranny-guest-essayist-james-c-clinger/. Accessed Dec 15, 2023.

Gueniffey, Patrice. *Bonaparte: 1769–1802*. Cambridge: Harvard University Press, 2015.

Jarus, Owen. *Who Was Napoleon Bonaparte?*. Live Science (2021). https://www.livescience.com/napoleon-bonaparte.html. Accessed Jan 09, 2024.

Scurr, Ruth. *Napoleon: A Life Told in Gardens and Shadows*. New York: Liveright, 2021.

Trouillard, Stéphanie. *Napoléon: Tyrant or genius - or both?*. France 24 (2021). https://www.france24.com/en/france/20210502-napoleon-tyrant-or-genius-%E2%80%93-or-both. Accessed Jan 10, 2024.

Zamoyski, Adam. *Napoleon: A Life*. New York: Basic Books, 2018.

Bonus!

Thanks for supporting me and purchasing this book! I'd like to send you some freebies. They include:

- The digital version of *500 World War I & II Facts*

- The digital version of *101 Idioms and Phrases*

- The audiobook for my best seller *1144 Random Facts*

Scan the QR code below, enter your email and I'll send you all the files. Happy reading!

Find more of me on Amazon!

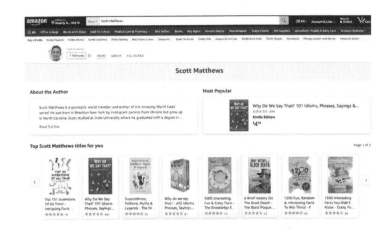

Check out the "Amazing Facts" series and learn more about the world around us!

Check out the "Why Do We Say That" series and learn where everyday idioms and phrases come from!

Made in the USA
Columbia, SC
02 December 2024

48204096R00059